LAWLESS WOMEN

BY COMMON CONSENT PRESS is a non-profit publisher dedicated to producing affordable, high-quality books that help define and shape the Latter-day Saint experience. BCC Press publishes books that address all aspects of Mormon life. Our mission includes finding manuscripts that will contribute to the lives of thoughtful Latter-day Saints, mentoring authors and nurturing projects to completion, and distributing important books to the Mormon audience at the lowest possible cost.

LAWLESS WOMEN

Heather Harris Bergevin

BCC
PRESS

For information contact
By Common Consent Press
4062 S. Evelyn Dr.
Salt Lake City, UT 84124-2250

Cover design: D Christian Harrison
Cover illustration: Curtis Jensen
Book design: Andrew Heiss

www.bccpress.org

ISBN-13: 978-1-948218-02-3
ISBN-10: 1-948218-02-X

10 9 8 7 6 5 4 3 2 1

For Donna and Latham Harris
who birthed and raised me at least twice

For Evva, Ammon, and Elias,
who I always choose first, every day,
and always will

And for J. Grady Locklear,
who gave me kind words in perilous times,
and told me to keep writing poetry

Contents

Introduction

My editor said I needed to write you a letter introducing myself and my poems, "explaining what the poems are about, how I came to write them, whether I ever drink the blood of young children in pagan earth-mother rituals. You know—that sort of thing." I told him that I'm feminist, and I keep hearing that that's what we do, despite my protests of denial. I cannot possibly condone drinking the blood of young children. It's far too unhygienic, and I've studied too much about blood borne illness in the past twenty years, even if you set aside the issue of children and consent. I don't generally do earth-mother rituals either, unless you count reading under trees in orange hammocks, which might be a form of worship.

Still, a couple of words of introduction might help.

I fell in love with mythology when I was viciously reading my way through my fledgling elementary school library. Andrew Lang's Fairy Books somehow fell into my lap, and became manna to my tiny, hungry eyes. Thinking back, those editions were probably a sadly abridged variations of his individual books, but the stories endured. I felt like I was reading a secret code, one where the carefully curated tales read to us in classes were much more raw and real. I had no idea that Goldilocks was originally a silver haired old woman, that Medusa got a raw deal, and that variations of Cinderella date back thousands of years, including the versions related to Shakespeare's King Lear. As I grew, I discovered that the original Grimm stories were much moreso, and even Greek Mythology had more than one source available. It never occurred to me in childhood, though, that Zeus was a jerk, or that Juno might have good reasons for feeling bitter, though she directed her actions poorly. I feel rather ashamed that it took me decades to realize that most, if not all, of those mythologies were taken directly from the words of men, mostly older scholars and researchers. I don't want to diminish that—it is good work, transcribing the words told at hearths, firesides and bedsides, and especially when those tales could be lost. They tell us so much about anthropology, history, cultural interaction. I felt robbed, though, upon realizing that these stories, which had been told and retold for generations by all people, were mostly written down only through the perspective of and analyzed through the languages of men. When did the elderly midwife, slowly supplanted by medical science she was denied, shift from being the strange old woman who makes herbal remedies, into the crone or witch to be feared for her primitive potions? Why is any woman educated in a monastery suddenly suspected of wizardry and seen as dangerous? Why were the stepmothers and queens always evil? Does history originate from and get written about only one gender?

Does the voice of the storyteller matter?

I am honored that you are choosing to read my words. I hope that you enjoy them.

Fondly,
HB

Disclaimer

Nothing in any of these poems is supposed to be about anybody specifically, except maybe the few pieces about my kids when they were little, and the one about my grandmother. I'll be highly surprised if she complains, though, as she passed away and is much happier now.

Otherwise, if you think it's about you, I apologize—mostly because it's not, and you're going to be disappointed that it wasn't. Sorry in advance.

Lawless Women

There are women, rebellious
against/with a turgid patriarchy,
who have lost much more than I,
who have given more. The ones
who locked away their
own Rapunzels, to forcekeep
them from participation in this
new religion, newly immigrating, in
this trek west, some second
wife, mail order. The ones who trekked, lost
lives (their own, their children, buried)
shawlwrapped,
under predator deterring stones?
What lives are lived
in quiet, patient desperation,
where law nor God approves
of your womanhood? What hope
redeems when God Himself abandon(ed/s)
and all is lost?
Does yet she come, that
Shekiniah gift, this
Goddess of trees, whose dead children
he hews to build our homes?
What desecration
sanctification
have we forgotten, we
Lawless women,
redeemed by God, abandoned by
man and men and authority
of men?

First

Eve was first.
Second born, maybe—she had that
second born's drive.
First born is dominant, second competitive,
they tell us in psychology courses.
The troublemaker and peacemaker
come later, naturally. So she was
second—but first
to partake, and probably
first to name—you know
she had a favorite civet-cat or
giant sloth, manatee or
somesuch. First
scientist, botanist,
critical thinker, humanist
empirically minded,
first communication driven, seeking
to share her fruited understanding,
　　　shake worlds with her
knowledge and experience. First
teacher. First to see
the good goal to receive
knowledge being greater
than stunted growth, first
remembering the Glory
of God is intelligence. . . . Was she first
to leave? First clothed to hide
the fullness of her woman's body, first
to pray, beg her Father, Mother not to leave

her alone, entirely? First to pursue
the never ending quest for science
for knowledge, to make
History.
First betrayed. First hated.
First forgotten.

(with regards to Bryce Blankenagel)

Vashti

The queen refused and so
the call went out throughout all the land (well
not so much a call or audition, per se, more
demand) Let all youngbeautiful, the virgins (hymens
priced above the glistening rubies
be gathered, paraded before the
guy in charge of testing
they were still intact, and making
sure the reason they were virgins
wasn't actually because they're ugly,
stupid, or diseased,
For such a time as This,
after a year in the palace,
alone, bereft of God
the new concubine
Esther won the favor
of her sex trafficker, her owner
The Noble King, and won
her crown, persistently keeping
her head down, submissive
loveliness in love (well, for
a while), beautiful
orphan jewess (hidden things),
uncle visiting late (hidden
messages: do not despair,
do not give up. Do not tell them. I know
it's difficult). They value
your proclaimed former purity only
for the joy of capturing it.

I wonder did she think
upon the Queen Vashti, paraded
naked in her crown before
the drunken jeering
men perhaps one too many
times, refusing of their rights to
witness of her loveliness bought
by masterking? We don't know
where she went—or did she die—killed
for insolence? Or, merely
Crown taken for her prideful
disobedience? Was she relegated
deep into the harem quarters
away from nubile ears that listen
to disobedient queens? Or could she
whisper encouragement and counsel
to her beautiful successor
teaching queenly manners, refusals
how to give enough and yet
Not give in.

Ease of the Way
Being Mormon isn't hard
when you are Normal.
If you are, well,
Seronormative
    average, regular—
        just-a-guy, you know?
Cis.
Het.
Not too smart . . .
I don't mean *disabled*,
That's not easy, I'm not saying it is,
we don't even have enough
parking spaces, one or two
on each side of the chapel. That gets filled
by the old people pretty fast, so
there's probably not room for your wheelchair.
It's super easy, though,
as long as you're not depressed,
because then you're depressing, and nobody
wants to be around depressing people—
so make sure to smile and hide that,
while wondering who else
is doing the same
Don't have a child who has
ADD, SPD, ASD, or who just
Asks too many damn questions; we don't
want to distract the other children
from learning how to obey. We can
Deal with all that, really—

Inconveniences, trifles.
You can be female. I won't complain.
Black, even, Mexican,
(Don't tell me if you're one of them
undocumented kind, OK?)
Shoot, you can even have
a queer kid (but not
Too queer). We support equality
in the workspaces and housing, we're
totally progressive like that. As long as you don't, like,
you know, make it
super obvious. Or like
promote it or anything. It's
Just so Simple:
Be married (but not to anyone
abusive, and in the temple, don't be divorced and)
Be Happy, (but not fake happy,
and not the kind that comes
from sinning and) Be Righteous,
Be Studious, but not
anything we didn't give you to study,
and not history
or older doctrine
or what we said that we don't say we
said about stuff we don't really
want to think about. Be Good.
It's simple. And, if possible,
be a guy.

Haircut

you come to me in tears, saying, "too hot
I can't even brush it anymore,
just cut it off." But we,
I falter, can go down the block
and get a special cut, this afternoon.
I worry my chances of doing it
right, straight, perfection
all those tiny hairs in the sink—no,
you stay resolute, You. We go
into the bathroom, and tie back
your Godiva tresses, twelve,
fourteen curly inches. Everyone says
they want my hair, mom,
you smile, maybe I should just
give them a wig of it. I cut across
the top of the rubber band—it takes
three passes to cut the full
thickening of your curls. The hair falls across
your face as I cut, amateur, as if I'm making
and embarrassing mistake, when you
start giggling in gleeful joy, Look!
Oh mom, Look!
It parts perfectly, curls gracefully, dives to your chin
waves diagonal, uneven
perfection.

I trim tiny snips from the back
and neck, while you grin in
the mirror, instantly older, instantly taller,
beautiful (but you were

always beautiful.) I look
Older! Oh Mama, Thank You! Oh!
We decorate with curl spray, scrunchies and
your excitement.
It occurs to me, this trustwalk,
you never faltered at my
fledgeling ability, and while
your belief sustains, it is
but is not
only hair.

Gothel

I.

Owner of my own business,
two homes (one vacation)
do my own work, gathering, gardening
(and am good at it, too)
can read, midwife, mix herbs and potions
for pain, for labor, for illness, and though
I prefer herbologist,
of course they think
I'm a witch.
Especially because I
read and write, but refuse,
obstinately, to be cloistered,
wed to God, which
makes no sense, even
to me, except I
would love to get my
hands on all those
books.

Thirteen hundreds already and I have
no husband, no fifteen
children, am not prematurely
grizzled to a gray crone
from working for a family of thirty extended
relatives—livestock mucked, kids
mucked, husband mucked—
(so they see my lack
of wrinkles and gray as magic,
naturally)

There are advantages to being vegetarian,
gardening instead of mucking
and I didn't ask for this kid
(though I longed and ached
for her), but it seemed silly, some guy
showing up, his idiot wife
convinced she'd die
for lack of what? kale?
a pregnancy craving? and he just
offered his kid, in lieu of his wife—
here, have my kid, so my wife will not die
from pregnancy craving. Could have asked
for the folic acid, iron, for the greens, but, no.
I figured
this baby'd be better off,
than where it'd be taught no
basic nutrition, reading, where it'd be
either as stupid as its father or mother
when just a little basic education
would make a world open to it.

Then it was a girl, this babe,
and neither parent cared, preferring
to try again for oldest son
rather than dowered daughter.
So I delivered
a healthy baby girl.
They said she died and tried
again for their desired firstborn
son. I gave them a gift:
rampion in a pot, for remembrance, but they

forgot anyway, in the end (when she grew, lovely, smart
educated in herbs and greens and mixtures
of essential oils and poultices, well spoken,
well dressed by my hard work of
witching in the world) remembering
only thieving crone.

II.
I counseled the king, of
course, traveling miles
to greet him with my wares
upon his throne. I think he likes
having an intelligent, strong, educated
woman—if a woman, he said, you
surprise me, Gothel, your debate and
logic equal nearly
a man's (after I'd beaten him
at chess, of course . . . we must
save face). He pays me,
well, for the services I provide
in lieu of intelligent queen. I loved him,
once.

His son is loyal, handsome,
vapid (naturally), well versed
in stabbing and shooting and killing
large and small mammals
of two legs and four. He hunts often,
posing on a white stallion,
glistening armor, (horrid breath)
ribboned sleeves embroidered,

six or seven tokens up his sleeve.
Just the kind of idiot an undereducated
equally vapid, hormonal girl
(sick of listening to wandering bards
sing on their lyres of mystic romance,
love potions, unicorns, and other
drivel), longing for their own
pretended romance, own
fifteen children, one or two each year,
would love. Stupid things,
who know not what princes are,
(loyal, brave and true, always, for at least
a couple of years). That's the type
that would expect you to be content
to sit and sew and coo at babes
and never make anything, or learn, or
grow, or create
anything but dinner, clean linens, fed
chickens, more babies—

III.
Not this child. She will grow and learn
and have all—safe home, educated husband, babes
if she wants them, garden, shop,
potions magic and book magic
(which is more powerful anyway)
and all I can offer. He had better
take no early liberties or trick
her into marriage. I would have
to kill him, or at least try. No out of wedlock

babes for my child, no shame in his
playing becoming her
infidelity, her "mistake." They'd call me
a witch for that, indeed, protecting
my treasured child, from what?
a prince? a dullard? a
thief? liar?
. . . royalty may be all that
and promiscuous, too.
I should know.
after all, he is
my son.

Lawless

I.

You think of me that woman
lawless, Brigham's concern,
refusing common
sense, intending
revelation unto herself.

Thank God.

II.

Do you think you are a one
mighty and strong, made
to set this house in order,
alone prophecy
as others failed to counsel
you in ways you were indeed
willing to follow?
The prophets speak
to you in riddles
from the dust,
joying you,
cursing me, your fun
damentalist heart
rejecting all
counsel not your own.

Some Children

There are some children I
cannot abide. Their constant
pressing, pressing chatter,
refusal of bedtimes refusal
of boundaries, refusal of
obedience, and only one of them
was me—the loud child, too smart by half,
(or thought she was), too lost
in day dreams and focused on
birds outside windows to realize
her annoyance to others. An
Acquired Taste. And suddenly, one day I
know, that taste (not for everyone), is still
useful, umami, the unfamiliar
spice that resonates at back of the
soft palate, not further
forward, like tabasco, but deep
like tamarind and hot curry—and
It's ok that not everyone likes
those things. There are thousands who
seek out those flavors, search out the strange
new fruits in foreign lands, want to know
if durian gags, if the flavor of
ants differs from region to region, while some
are content with one variation
of red apple and grocery store
peaches. You go on and enjoy
your standardized children, your standardized
testing, your standardized lives—but if

someday, perhaps, you want to learn
about 500 variants of apples, alone,
in North America, and that some
Patagonian potatoes taste
strongly of strawberries, and grow
in colorful clusters like underground grapes:
you find me. Acquire. We will sup
together.

Stepmother

1.

I wasn't, you know.
Wicked.
I wasn't her step
mother, either—she was my own
tiny doppelganger, sweet faced
Peaches and cream and roses baby,
round eyes peering blue up
from suckling breast. I married
young, was widowed young (the wars,
you know), remarried
young again. He had
a couple of babes, too, our blended
family creating that stepping
stone in my name, Grimm given. But, oh,
how I loved her, gorgeous
bone of my bone of my flesh
and she grew, tall, willowy, supple, as I
grew older, her breasts
budding as mine faded, her
porcelain complexion pale against
my dead love's Spanish hair, and I grew
nervous, as the king, he lost
interest in me, while glancing at
his comely, innocent step
daughter, who continued more
pallid as she saw his royal
limpet gaze saying, come, girl, let's
have a song, come sit

here on my lap.
I sent her away. They said
jealousy. I say self
preservation, for my own life, and that
of my girl, who soon
will start her moons and grow,
magically mirror
mirroring myself
six babes and this long decade past.
I sacrificed a boar to
the goddess, and sent my
dearest friend (ok, and
lover) to deliver my treasured
child to the labor faction
deeply forested.

2.
When I say dwarves, you think
more twee than Tolkein
(Forget Disney). I mean
hardened, mine-worked men,
artisans in metallurgy,
jewelers to Europa
(before that was a thing, even).
Adept hunters, trappers,
mountaineers, who just happen
to be tall as my elbow, and
terribly strong. A
single dwarf can mine
hours without tiring, fight

bears off their livestock, make
chainmail fine as silk that still
stops arrows, and that before breakfast.
It behooves a princess
to work a good while, her
elbows up in suds, her
feet stinking from mucking out,
hefting an axe.
Soft hands can ruin and return,
but the mind stays hardened,
learning more than needlework
and Latin, learning the
ways of women and men.
We used to send our Royal
children in trades to apprentice
in their betrothed's household, to play
together, live, learn each other's
minds while innocent. This is merely
secondary apprenticeship to life.

3.
How she rejoiced
to see her mother, old and bent
with age and art (half pretended)
when I came visiting.
I brought her
presents, tokens twice—first
a comb, engraved, her father brought me
from foreign travels, and, later
apples, saved from banqueting,

secreted in my bosom for later
eating. I had thought my disguise
effective enough, my co-
conspirators silent, but Oh,
to see her choke and clutch
that white neck, to see the apple
fall, snake persuasive betrayal.
My warrior friends inconsolable, blaming
me, for bringing accursed
fruit. I thought her dead,
and at my hand—no difference:
the king had found
out my subtle deception.
My daughter, life,
away, draining.

4.
What potion, spell or
prayer could protect her
now? Her rescue a
resurrection, brought
hand and mouth by her passing
former play-friend. The king
is dead of apple tart, long live
the king, the queen mother needs some
time to ponder starts and restarts, time
to brew, and make, and reform.
Let them think
what they will.
I have saved my own.

Colossians
you tell me to speak yet
be silent
to defend, but not
the innocent.
you ask me to find my voice
and say my heart,
but carefully in only the right
tone
and not in classes,
or online,
or in the home,
or community,
so do (but don't), unless
it's what we say to say to say.
you tell me my life has meaning
purpose, direction, the right
to agency, to revelation
in my callings, my world, but
only the approved meaning
purpose
direction, agency
you choose and I seem to
begin to see that all
things and people are equal, just some
are still, after all
these years, more
equaller than others, and you say
Speak, Sisters!
And I speak,
and you read to me
Colossians.

Joann

Practicing your favorite song
for the funeral,
I recall testimony of your faith
strength courage sass
canning, sewing, each relief
Society meeting. My first
ward friend, my example
of intellect with firmness,
Kindly, gently not
suffering fools, teaching
ever, pain ever, optimism
ever. Your daughter said
your witness was your hope
that they would see you in
your Priesthood in
the temple, by and by.
Amen, amen
from your lips, to the Greatness
of God's love,
and all your sister's
future hopes for greeting
thus, amen.

Esther
Namesake,
It will be hard for those
        to whom you speak Truth.
They will say you are
sanctimonious, preachy, forceful,
smart (when you shouldn't be),
unapproachable, unshakeable,
unwavering—they mean you to
        Stop It.

            Don't.

They might rather live in
smoke filled opaque
glad glass villages,
befouled windows mocking eyes,
tacitly, politely conspiring
(agree to disagree) and sipping
mint juleps on the veranda:
fanning themselves, talking of
economic matters, clutching pearls and
getting vapors. They would not
have marched with Malcolm.
Would not have hidden slaves or
Jews in the basement. They pretend
slavery ended long ago, and trafficking
is something with cars, and anyway
        only happens elsewhere.
            And here you are—
squeegeeing windows,

asking transparency.
How can they s(k)ulk happily
in their soot soaked lovelyhouses
if you keep doing That?

Troy

Agamemnon lies—his little
war, littler honor, little
feet tested by gods, the ships stalled,
waiting whether by the blowing
hot air from Poseidon's pleasure
or his own, the warrior vowing
he would reach for Troy, to rescue
that trollop Helen, who, running,
far from her spartan surroundings,
Spartan king, that Menelaus,
(cursing Troy, cursed Paris, cursing
love or lust or fame, whichever,)
called his thousands, legions waiting
(im)patiently upon the shoreline.
Agamemnon lies, her knowing
of his lies, perhaps, and having
children thrice by liar, knowing
even royals get some warning
of impending death or marriage—
Agamemnon lies—in reading
"quick wife, send our oldest daughter,"
figured out the code for, "ok,
really, not a marriage so much
as a sacrifice," and warned her
patient daughter Iphigenia—
good Gods do not hate their daughters—
sent instead a suckling donkey
for the father's cruel appointment,
and the wind blew on regardless,

and the men (de)scribe her history—
killing patient Clytemnestra
(waiting vengeful for a decade
waiting with her cruel lover
for returning king and country), bringing
back the tricked Cassandra,
who had hoped that faithless lover
who had showered her with pleasures,
finally would wed her, bed her.
found instead an angry kingdom—
faced her fate with resolution,
knowing full her story twisted—Agamemnon lies.

Furball
Her voice was ever gentle,
soft and low, well,
hey, she'd been trained that way from
well born birth, to spelunking death and
really wasn't he just hopeful, projecting upon her
his desire for her future quiet, submissive life,
            but she was defiant,
tenacious,
little, fierce—they intended
submission, but got
subversion.
Confusing to her sisters, bitter
king, country, but still will
Rise up, dress golden
as the sun, shining
as the moon, glittering as
the stars, tiny spinning wheel
hiding in a walnut shell. Working
all day, dancing
all night, her salvation in soup.
You can't
hold down this tiny, filthy,
many furred mammal hiding
quietly in a tree, sleeping, stirring, trapped
by hounds, trapped by
toxic patriarchy expecting
her cleanliness, quietness, docile
submission. Well, mad King—someday
you'll come begging for

forgiveness, for scraps
of food and love. And she
will dive into her careful stores,
instructing all the bakers trained, to
reduce the salt, not for
cholesterol or Cordiality,
but regal consideration
of old man's years, fears. Her sister
betrayers not interested in
heretic geriatric regret,
ring once dropped in King's soup safe secured
upon her finger, her father's blind
blinded eyes sighted, and who will give
Notice
once again he is rescued
from royal stupidity by
Fierceness love, not gentle
complicity

Shadowed

I'm eldest, and let me
tell you, that's
no easy business, that:
being eldest, and a
girl, here at the turning
of a brand new century. London
or New York, it is the same: grow
up, debut rich, dance much,
practice flirting, practice
household budgeting,
childcare. Tonight,
it's me watching
my silly little brothers
(bothers) and dog, while
they have date night—fancy
dress even, Mummy looking
delicious, darling, Daddy putzing
about and blaming
her for his crooked tie.

If anything I've got
four? five years? before coming
out bold, with the edict: Don't
Disappoint Daddy.
Silly Daddy, scooting about
thinking he knows a hawk from
a handsaw, man of business—
can't find his own
cufflinks, and blames mummy, who
isn't supposed to know

anything, can't vote,
but is lovely and finds
all the cufflinks one needs.

I figured one good
story before bed, one last
weaving of words before
lying dreamily thinking
of gauzy gowns and frustrated
courtiers. How could I know—
one kiss, it couldn't be
a big deal, right? Merely
on the cheek proffered.
How could I know the binding
spelled upon that kiss?
So small and knobbly in the hand,
so simple and light to hang
around the neck, a souvenir,
a noose?

It would save my life,
and lose it, loose it,
unfettered bobbing
over the cathedral heights
of the shuttered-eye windows, second
on the left and on
until morning. The brothers
came too—a lady always
needs chaperones, and
little ones must do. You can't
wait, when you

look into the face of an
eagle, golden, the face
of a faun, of Oberon's
friend, of Tempest's
creator and know at once
that it is your own
twin soul's face, and offer
not just cheek,
but hand, but heart.
I felt I aged
six years in a sprinkling
of glittered magic, of
grudgingly given hope.

I'd asked my mother once,
fussing over a boy at school,
if they ever grow up, ever. Without
a word she led me
into the back garden, where
Daddy and the boys were playing
at being red Indians. I wondered
if Indians
play at being me, and
thought I might not
like that, actually. I wonder
if they do, far away out
west beyond the sea, or if
our play, offensive, concerns.

All the girls here who
could (should, might)

be my friends, just
flip their tails, fly away, and
will not,
so beautiful is this boy,
crowing like a rooster—yet,
I stay, and he builds
(or causes to be built)
me a little house
to keep our family in. I know
eversomany stories
and he always keeps me
safe, from any danger, so
it's not until I realized
suddenlike, that when
he calls me Mother, he
doesn't mean it like Daddy does,
calling Mummy like a title,
like a priestess in her kingdom,
but Mother like my youngest
brother calls in his sleep
for home. I hear her fair(l)y
tinkling laughter,
having won, at my
recognition, knowing
my bubble broken
cannot be repaired
with clapping, with
happy thoughts, with
pixie dust, and I am going
Home—younger,

older, wiser, foolish
to hope it could all be
unlo(i)ved, once seen.

How was I to know
such a kiss is binding? So,
child, when he comes,
looking exactly the same as
a god, swooping to
carry your heart away
with soapy heels and
red feathers—don't you go.
You will regret it.

Winged

We are in the car, and he says
"Mom, did you know
bats are ancestors of
dragons?" I restrain my untoward
laughter, ask
"Bats are? But why?"
He explains scientifically—1,
their wings are the same, 2, they both
like enclosed spaces, 3, (he is holding
a small black polymer beastie now) they both
scare people but can be
very sweet, when you know them.
"They are Roomates!" he exclaims, delighted at
this epiphany, "in caves!"
He fingers the face of the tiny treasure,
and I ponder his own emerging wings
and fire, hiding from his fears under the
spare bed, behind the
moving boxes, and long
for his small scaled self to flee
far from the constant misperceptions of his
too strong, too wiggly, too bouncy,
little furry, snuggly dragon self
that others also call Monster.

Pieta

we always think of the mother, don't we, not
father standing holding empty coffee cup, not
sibling sitting at bedside, but always Mother
    marble and cold
weeping, ever weeping, cradling the body of her
broken son. Thank Michelangelo.
Well distanced, we—mother, father, sister, not
Mark and Louise, Anne and David, the Body, not
John.

our feebled protection—
to travel, look upon the marble statue, see
    the cradled son, weeping marble
(far behind velvet ropes) tour guides intoning
    "this is death, please do not
    touch, the oils from your
    fingers will mar the masterpiece," and yet
that distanced shattered, first name only,
    we get attached
to these frail forms—as we are
all broken, all chose this destination, too
soon or too late.

What else is there but to love
deeply and to hurt
greatly, lose
completely? Protection from
betrayal is protection
from hope. Is there any final
betrayal like that of lungs

failed, drowned in fluid, heart
stopped.
upon a cross of hospital bed—
it is the same (and my heart with yours).
Soon they will come to bind you
away, in a week, maybe more, nobody
will speak your name to me, tell our stories, lest
they cause me grief.

Did His mother, too, receive hall
mark cards of how this child, perfection, is better
off for having lived and
died, and how someday will live,
which does no more than cause
my vigil keep
three days, five days, seventy years . . . and
an intense desire to slap
the letter writer.
If I hear again how God never
gives us more than we can
handle, trite platitudes,
our promise only of balm eventual not
sudden and sweet at coffin
close and final hymn,
handshake, vacummed hall, tossed kleenex
and collection of
pyrex, clean, sometime next week.

There is too much death in living,
        too much living in death,
no marble hand to hold, impossibly cold and

sculpted with tears.
Empty, cup empty,
bed belongings to hold and smell, pack and mourn,
people who need
comforting by we, The Bereaved, who must be told
their frail attempts at comforts are comforting,
well suited, lest they also
retreat hiding from the specter at the potluck.
We are all specter
at life, and yet deny our spectacular coming. We hide
from those unable to hide
that intent, to sometime have audacity to die.
And yet
we are born to die, some sooner,
some more sudden, all messily
as we came.

La belle dame

"Sans merci" they called you—
woman, you fascinate me.
Beauty, sprite, rowan,
were you born changeling
with this lack, without the gifted
Theory of Mind? As so many
around me, surround me, I wonder, did you
wander, chameleon, to become
whichever thing was needed, mirroring
necessity to get by? Or did he think
you mirror, when it was
his projected face he saw? Was it indeed gentle
sociopathy enhanced by beauty? Those
knights constantly falling over themselves
for your life giving visage, before losing
their lives to you—or were you pained
like we, a woman filled brimming
with mercy, empathy, worry, being
used and used and used and used
up, until we find that cup
of human kindness dry, adrenal fatigue?
You intrigue
even me, belle dame sans merci.

Tuesday,
Wake long in time to
bathe before taking
kid to class early, wait,
and drive home to
dress the first grader, ready
all others, backpacks and
homework, then
Shoe all like ponies, race
Headlong front lawn,
Buckles and prayers and
Gain school in just time for
Tardy bell first toll and
call to swap daughter's new
dental to early,
avoiding the late fee, then
race past the dentist
and off to buy shower
gifts, but see blue lights
out giving tickets, so
daughter to dentist and go
fix the brake light
before there's chastisement,
on procedures broken, then
back, to grab daughter, and set up
appointments for fillings and sealants, wrap
presents together and
drive to the shower, with
pound cake for toasting, to
sit

play with babies, share
munching on sweetmeats, when
daughter gets headache, so
leave to run errands. Get home
in just time to
meet son bellicose from
mean kid on in his bus ride, explain
to the driver, you know and
she's always
most welcome to call,
if any confusion—then race
to the homework, remembering lastly
to grab seventh grader and drop
return package
in dropbox at Pilot, to get
home exhausted and
suddenly realize
It's only three-forty, and I'm so
exhausted, still—
catfood's forgotten.
Be right back.

Medea

Everyone in history is all angry that I
killed my own, my children. They've
forgotten—history is written by the
ones who live to write it and who have
enough power to get the scribes to say
what it is they want for them to say, and boy,
does Jason have all that in spades: handsome, witty,
charismatic, he came out
smelling like a rose, didn't he?
Who got the fleece? Who escaped Theseus, sacrificed
everything
for love, for love, who
sang to sleep the giants, the wyvern, the
robot guardian? But, no, I am
that witch—he, the philandering
bigamist, Heroic. People name
their children after
him, not me.
Beguiled, loved, trusting—I once
used all my power(s) for this now
kingly fool. His poisoned life, wife, burning castle I
don't regret. So when he sees
me wipe blood from my hands, holding fast
the reigns, nodding towards small
blood soaked prone bodies in the
wagon behind, he will not follow, having
been thoroughly b(w)itched. It will be
hours before he finds the slaughtered
goats, still longer before his mind rises, hazed,

remembering that lolling song and singer which causes
beasts and men to sleep
as if in death.
By then, we will escape,
far to harbor and sea and shore, away and no
body will look for Medea and her children,
as there is no more of either. But history
will erase: the king, bereft by his
witch ex, not betrayed princess but only
malevolent murderess.
I will not care.
Let them say as they will. I will run
with my own in sunlit fields Elysian, far
from Argo, from Jason, and his children
will be free to remember
or not remember
as they please.

Seafoam

distanced from parents,
ever obedient
popping face above
surfaces of new worlds, your
story of abused abusive love,
obsession. Body cleaved
severely severed, walking on
razors, eggshells, giving up
your sister's companion love for piece
of souleternity, possibly
redemption. His betrayal the more
intensely intensity, physical cursed
pain fade following physical
metaphysical betrayal—sweet foundling, his
fondling touch
belonging to another, her given kingdom,
face haunting, his mouth
whispering her name. Little one, you do need
your sister's feminine beautysacred
hair shorn, traded
to dagger, then dagger for
memory. Daughter of the air, I would not
be as kind with knives
suffer more pain to please him
while he does not recognize
any portion of your nature or
sacrifice. I count
your tears, for naughty children,
and men, to see your life
sold for a ship's dowry.

High Functioning in the Victorian Period
Bartleby would prefer
Not to eat new foods
Not to leave the house
Not to go to stores.
Bartleby would prefer
Not to read aloud,
Not to check his work,
Not to change routine.
Bartleby would prefer
Not to be disturbed
Not to shield his eyes
Not be spoken to.
Or about.
Or around, and
Bartleby would prefer
To be left alone
(But not actually alone) with
Constant care of children bearing
Gingerbread production
For his sensory standardization.
Bartleby would prefer
Not to go outside
Not to be bombarded
With noise and cats and beer
And pubs and children, hansom
Carriages clatter in the street, and
Bartleby would prefer
Not to go on living
Faced with all the challenges, he
Would prefer not to.

Isabella Eleanor to Perrault

Look
here's the thing: I'm not
that forgettable. I've been
known to turn heads, even
in rags, even wearing
the most uncomfortable of
shoes and clothes—I'm just
a looker. And yet,
there it is—he couldn't
identify my face in a crowd,
even a crowd of one, couldn't
describe my nose, my eyes,
though he can see them.
Yet, he fell
almost on sight, in love,
(face blindness not being
diagnosable in these
sixteen hundreds.) I don't mind—
wouldn't you rather, after
decades of being memorable
for Prettiness (Such
a nice face), pettiness talking
behind your back, to instead
know with absolute certainty
he loves your mind? It's
not like he can't see
my facial features, but can't ever
remember specifics. I change
my hair, he might pass

accidentally by me, his wife,
in the street—except my soul, my vocal
cadence, lilt, my ideas, ideals, my style,
the way I hold my shoulders, those
cannot be hidden by voluminous
skirts or new court styles and wigs.
and really,
isn't it better, to love a mind, a heart,
a soul, rather than prefer
a face and a Venetian
glass slipper.

Bird
In the corner of my garage
was you, my little bird.
Fluffed out.
Tail braced.
Face deep into the corner,
hdng.
I thought you were dead.
I thought your fluff was, maybe,
all remaining of your
brief, tender life.
I tried to shine a light
upon you, but you were so high
above on the tiny ledge;
you didn't notice,
in your solitude.
I thought you
were dead, yet in
the morning you were
goneflown. Perhaps
you sorted your fluff
straightened your tail,
unfaced that
hidden upmost corner
and flew away.
My sonbird, do not
flyfar, hide cornered.
Come back to me.
Here,
there is food.

Lesser God

There is a god of wasted things—
butterflies upon the wing, who
draft into antennas, splat—
sabbath friends and things like that.

An alto's voice, a felted skein,
tomato spot on windowsill,
fit shoes (one lost), that jog at dawn,
rejected ring, a necklace spilled
with bead tumbled upon the green—
there is a god of wasted things

which, proffered, offered silver tray
binged netflix shows from pain, days lost,
when set aside, further decay—
and loves, and infancy, and frost—

he packs them neatly—one lost sock,
the keys to homes rejected, lost
the child unborn, the time untaught,
degree left halved because of cost,
a twisted arm, their childhood caught—
his packages unopened, frost
-ed with greed, desire shrill,
there is a god of wasted things
from nothing but our pride or will.

Issues

untouchable—twelve years
infertile in Christ, unable to serve
in gospel, temple,
to work towards cleansing,
because the blood
will   not   stop,   cannot
cease and who
can help or heal or offer remedy,
medicine, herbs, to a woman
bleeding, plagued, bleeding
with issue of blood? They tell me
I must never
touch anyone
lest they, too, become
unclean, untouchable, shunned, voiceless,
contaminated by my obvious sin
and lack of faith
to be healed. But I've heard a God
walks among us, speaks,
and heals with his touch—I cannot
ask him to touch me, to become
willingly tainted
to choose to be branded
pariah. Could I?
The pain is too great, the doctrine
of shunning unclean things, the rituals
I cannot dance within or celebrate, too
critical to heaven and my
governors. I cannot inflict them

upon another. But what if
(could I?), hidden by the press,
low, in humility, reaching, reaching
if not knocked away,
if not too late,
if not kicked apart so as not to contaminate
the crowd of believers, I
stretched out
my spirit with my arm, to graze
the very corner of his robe. And hoped?
Could I?

Jacques-Bernard Brunius describes
Palais Ideal to the Dadaists
Cheval tripped on a rock
and it being pretty and
interestingly shaped, he
pocketed it, and others,
until, wearing holes into pockets
(at wife's complaint, this new obsession)
graduated up to baskets, collecting
hoarde upon hoarde
of plain old pebbles, boring, tiny
pieces of stone. He finally needed
wheelbarrows, gathering, gathering.
A wasp, he daubed
thick concrete, sculpted
dream prophecies into
mocked reality, though neighbors
whispered, (this mad, bedraggled, poor
fool postman, who fills his yard
with flowers made of stones.
Hauterives snickered, but foreign visitors came
touristing, encouraging, imbibing
this strange visual concoction arising dreamlike
over the French countryside.
Cheval, unaltered, undeterred, made a plaque
upon his fantastique concrete
cavepoolpalacesculpturecoraloctoputti
"With this rock," (it said), "I wanted
to prove what willpower
can achieve." He died

~~a ridiculed postman, architect, mason (besides~~
who isn't a bit of a mason,
he said) with phrases
script scrawled
throughout, a mantra: "The work
of one man. . . . Impossible
does not exist."

Juno Melania

They ask me why she stays, the
gold-digger. Brainless. She
asked for this, surely she
knew, before they married, long
before she bore his son, and won
the country's eyes and my
concern. I can't
explain properly, that she was
his newest, best loved
favorite plaything, beloved
honored, supported, treasured,
until his attention wavered. They don't
look right, abusers. Not Hollywood at all. No
refusal to shave, no waving guns around,

lunatic. They sound normal, mostly, their words mostly
          making almost sense. They don't hang out wearing
 sleeveless shirts, screaming Stella, leaving bruises
where others can see. They look like you. They are
kind, they are godly, and such good businessmen.
Except when they're not, but usually, that's not where you,
the public, can see.
Was it pregnancy, or after
birth he lost interest, moved to some new toy, and she
faded off to background noise, annoyance?
Did she then realize her
prenuptial (she never would need
because all his exes were crazy, not
him, and he love love loved her)
would bind securely, that he

~~could steal her son, as he stole~~
those other children from the first
two marriages renounced? Did he
threaten her with immigration
difficulties, twist any
little flaw or worry she had known
over their decade? Was their
son to need her balance, if she could
not escape? Is he well, or
his father's son, that apple not
falling far?
Maybe she knows enough to take him
at his word, that he will always
do everything he says he will,
and therefore, stays,
crushed empty, silent,
not even mistress of her own house,
supplanted. Maybe he's not her
First Abuser.
But, why does she stay, the damn'd
stupid gold-digger? When she
Obviously should go.

Optical

Leaves are green, or rather
they are anything except for green, as light
bounces back from their veined surfaces in any
wavelength excepting the one
seen in my eyes, which, tricked, confused
assume greeness, assume redness,
yellowness, orangeness, brown crunchiness in fall.
So when you come to me with careful
factually based arguments saying I
am black, you are white, I
am white, you are black,
these brown, these gold, these burnt umber, I
wonder where
you sourced your information, and whether
your correlation is reliable. Your experience, however,
never deceives the eye, bouncing back,
radially, your voice, ringing, that I am
too white, too black, too brown, and (I cannot
possibly understand, I know, and yet) I
confusedly, stumble about, thinking of rods and cones,
thinking of blues and greens and reds, optical nerves,
under the shadow of falling evening when no
color effectively matters, (yet provided by our memory
they persist, our brains fluid in consistency expecting naught
in changes) excepting that of skins and fear and
walking shadows in the darkness, and I
wonder if I can stop attempting to pretend
colorblindness, can stop explaining my own
perspective for sufficient
to begin expanding my capacity to
see light.

Mise en abysme

Staring in,
you see first:
flaws, these small
lines left by laughter,
zits that keep reoccurring
under that scar
at the edge of the nose.
the eyes are, well, ok,
right spacing, colour
not terribly boring. Bow
lips that would be
lovely, if not for
jowls, waddle—oh,
well.
This is what
we've got. Staring
in. Watching
change. Seeing
the abyss
stare back.

Nauvoo

How did it feel,
(house swept, china
cleaned and
shattered sparkling,
tokens taken, but curtains,
pianos, glass-paned windows,
sidewalksliliestrees and
gardens, books, treasures
left on sideboards, carefully
dusted, broom behind the door),
to walk in, w(a)ondering
this ghost town, ripe
for gleaning, looting in the
September sunshine, with
footsteps crackling still in the mud
flowing endlessly as a river
outward toward the West? I could come
and sweep your floors, tend your
gardens, but would they ever feel
to be my own stewardship? Or
changeling child, usurping the
crown of the little spinny angel
on top of the hill? It's just
stuff, after all, you were leaving
to me, like a little
surprise gift wrought
of terror, wrought of
helpless hope. My children
would play in your barn and

eat your chickens, not
knowing where
their wicked benefactors had gone
or if they ever found their sought
safe harbor.

Emotional Labor Day

I have come to visit, and
am watching my grandmother sleep. She
is peaceful, a large baby in a
navy denim dress. My father, her only child, is
out of town, so I
am substituting
for his infinite patience
with my vastly inferior kind. She
is so gentle, asleep. I almost forget
her screaming voice in the phone,
calling me spoiled, saying I
should have stayed with my husband. Saying I
am a brat, always have been. It is so quiet, perhaps I
can love her a little,
(while she is asleep), forget our trip
decades past on my birthday, when she first called me
Bitch.
What kind of life must you have, to be so creative, so
adventurous, traveling the world, meeting so many
fascinating people, and then to lie, day after day, in bed,
covered with hand crocheted lace coverlets, waiting
patientish to die? I wonder if I am seeing my
future, curled in place, refusing help, firing sitters,
remembering glories, eating and
voiding and little else. Will my grandchildren
fear me, dreading visits, hoping to sit next to me while
I sleep, instead of confronting our past
and future together? Will I pick
at souls and lace coverlets and

scream into the phone because I'm sure
my grandchild stole my Tylenol? Or lie and lie
peacefully asleep
in a denim dress.

Hyberbole

you don't blog? I can't believe
you don't blog! she trills
astonished, in my direction, I write
(she continues)
every day, all the cute
things they say, the sweet
pictures, all of it.
All? I say, do you? do you
write all? the dirt, the
hands that stink of pee, the
alfredo scalded to the pan,
whatever weird thing that was
the cat lay offering to you
as head of pride? The mummified
tree frog in the corner of your
unswept bedroom? all of it? She fumbles
well, no, they won't want
to remember all that stuff . . .
(then, brightening) I scrapbook, too,
all the pretty bits, the outings, awards, go here
color coded, acid free . . . (but I stare)
journal? do you journal? things you can write,
truths nobody
can see until long after
you're dead? OH, no, she says,
I blog. I can't believe you don't blog!
you should, you know, it's such a good way to
remember! We go back to our
class on family history

(she's teaching) and I wonder
in thirty years, will her daughter
smile at carefully chosen stickers
die cut, or mourn
because she cannot emulate
the ideal established by
her angel mother.

Magical Thinking and Sarcasm

If only while the shooter
carrying the automatic
AK47 pulsing/pushing bodily
past the front office(er,
uniformed, armed), if
only one dancing, joyous
crowd member had been
armed, if only he was not
muslim, christian, male
female, poor, rich, entitled, dis
enfranchised, if only they were
more like me (the victims, the
aggressors), if only gas prices were
higher/lower/solar, if
only the righteous survived, if only
the happy dancing people, if
only the good die young, if only they had more
time, responded faster if only
the investigators ended the conflict
more quickly (the dead
danced alone, lying faceless face down, phones) if
only the phones in their pockets would stop
ringing, ringing, as the beloveds
try to locate their dead.

On Sonnet 29

Remember when
we thought it was romantic love
the poet had, perhaps for her
(his dark lady) in these lines? That just
the thought of her,
arising in his heart, could dredge
away the poisoned looks of men?
Perhaps it's not, after all these
four hundred years and more, a
lark arising to think on thee,
but on Thee, on Thy love
to suffice the depths, instead.
Perhaps it is the same, love,
to suffer deaf heaven, to be wracked
with bootlessness, and cursing fate and yet
Go On,
love on, hope on, continue on
To choose to Be. And tomorrow
To choose again.

Rooted
You can't tell the strength of a thing until
it's broken, trees especially, upending
gale force winds exposing
all hidden detail, each root
balled into extreme detailed pressure
and forced into sunlight,
where it would not belong, except a peek
from digging squirrels or burrowing
nemotodeian army. The pines
go first—tall, proud, rigid in their
ways and growth and rings
soft wood, deep rooted, taproot down for ages, but they
snap, pressured too heavily. The winds
saying what they don't mean, screaming
down the alleyways of our minds, the pines
cannot sustain under force. The dogwoods, they dig
round, wide routings, losing limbs, but catch them
toohardtoolongtoodeep, their wide
flat systems, shallow, cannot sustain
Them
either, (while strong
Cellular structure, good genes, prevents cracking,

    falling
        over
and exposing one's undercarriage is just as
damaging,
in the long run).
You've got to have

both—deep
roots,and wide,
strength and twist
Both. Give me a live oak,
a magnolia, any day. They sway,
threaten to topple, then, right,
flex with ongoing
storm and pressure.
Maybe losing a little
off the top . . . but later, liveflourishgrow
again. The wind
becomes them—
as it does you, who are
roots in wind.

Consider
What kind of lilies grew
in fields just outside
of Jerusalem? I'd wager
not large petaled, flowy, showy,
people designed giants, white-waving
from caskets and sympathy cards, no—
smaller, wilier flowers,
scrubcloseclinging
to one another in that
overgrown field.

It's hard to be
a lily—wandering,
surviving on scrap minerals,
scraps of water other
plants discarded or accidentally
r(eig)ned upon you. Nobody thinks
about (considering) the lily—neither large
nor showy, and slightly
wild, but child
it does its own
Thing, and so
will you: Abandonment
never looked so good, never
was so strong, and long
before the lilies got to flower shops
and funerals, their cousins grew
free, fed by birds and clouds,
lived loud, tiny
proud lives in some
forgotten wilderness, deep within
Jerusalem.

Preschool

It was not six months ago
you asked the meaning of each phrase
(especially the ones you knew)
and learned at my knee/shoulder/side,
but now, so greatly wiser
the questions stop (except my own.)

how great the burden to know so much
so young, especially the grown wisdom
of my knowing so little. How should it be
that I no longer glimpse
when it is going to rain, if you will get
muddy, when you need to pee,
though you refuse,
muddy, wet from cold raining, dripping on
the floor from rainwater and urine?

will you add a zero and become
knowledgeable in your lack of knowledge,
teachable in humble again innocence, or remain
brilliantine genius, dripping platitudes
through the hall.

Tango

It takes two, you know
for a Lie. A lore
folk ripened for our damaging
needs two minds:
the liar, and the listenerbeliever. There has
to be, besides the one
seeking dishonesty, the one
seeking truth, and who would rather
hear truth where not present than
attempt to detect below
surface platitudes to read beneath. It
happens thus—the liar
Lies, whether intentional
or believing their own words, it is
the same damage in the end. The hearer, often
subject, always subjective, thinks
but surely
that was not what was meant,
and, deluded, carries onward, unless they begin
to question, "was this indeed what you meant?—the liar,
knowing
sociocultural boundary breaking
tends to get one deeply into
hot water, rejoins, "but
of course not, that could never be-
what those words mean is not
what they mean,
silly you.
The believer believes

until they don't, actually, and once
that leg is broken, even mended
holds the scar—each thing becomes
necessary analysis—do words mean
what we say they mean? Is my experience
not my experience? Is my world not my world not
my own existence? Believers doubt themselves,
not the liar, believe the goodness, not
any lying beneath. They slaughter
change, carefully explain, "well, we need
to make sure we reserve our judgement,"
and if they say Do you know
the fullstory? We need to offer up
unto the liar abuser
our common love, that they may
repent, you can be sure
the full story came
not from their eyes
not from their minds
not from research, or history, or sense
but from the liar, variation
being within his detection
his perception of himself
that he could never do this thing
he's done. So he did not.
and if you can have
the deceived visit your home,
and know them as individuals
and excuse the destruction of
their individuality? Of their perception of

Reality? Does this not indeed
make you complicit
to shifting your alliance, and indeed
your nature, into liar
from believer of lies.

Butterfly Soup

Butterflies begin
larval, munching, growing
moving constantly, forward then
halt
　　　　create a cave, personal
　　　　to hide, magicians all.

I have read that it is within
their slight, slick shells,
they disassemble all to slime.
sludge reforms: new eyes, new
legs, hard thorax and—most magical
wings they have never seen to copy,
from nasty stew, goop becomes
beauty (we call metamorphosis)

So when I see you, child
constantly munching, whirl of
motion, snuggly soft heart,
halt,
to hide sullen
in your headphones, reading
cocooned in the bottom bunk
of your room, I will
come to you, and
offer soup.

The West
boro Baptist church
teaches love
on Sunday, Monday
protests, big signs waving
rainbow colors, God Hates
Fags. You can read
interviews with their young
vibrant, kind, peaceful
members, just trying
to do as they have
been taught, to follow
as they have been always been
lead, to
always keep the Bible, keep their
lives pure.

We don't
hate gays, they attest,
God does, and we, His
humble servants, do
as he asks, in this protest
at the graveside of a
fallen soldier,
waving to the cameras. It's
about witnessing
for Christ, about defending the
families from the ongoing
onslaught of the insidious
gay agenda. We must
separate out

the wheat from the tares—
those who will follow,
those who will not follow. God's law,
not mine, not our own. If you
don't like it, you can just leave. It's
a free country.

In Colorado City they
teach love on Sunday,
Monday, Tuesday, but
only if you have
polygynous truths
embedded, wedded
bedded, rebedded—
Seed bearers called
as valiant servants,
wife upon wife upon
wife to breed
good seed, as
their husbands look on.
Keep Sweet, they explain, follow
your leaders, do
everything the scriptures
tell you to do (but only
our perfect translation) It's about
bringing up the faithful
to the Lord, you'll see—
are you wheat, or are you
tares? Are you brave enough to
Follow,
your leaders, your prophet

(though he be jailed)
over your instinct, your heart's
truth? "Stay on the Plan.
Hold, to the rod. And, can I
please
go walk alone with your daughter
to chat to get to know her
sweet spirit a little better.
(I will anyway, as your consent, or hers,
is in name only.)

We must defend our
families, against
the government, the others,
the prying praying eyes
that fight our God given cultural
(archaic) laws, and doctrine—let's
build
a wall to keep out
the world and keep in
all God's children
trying to escape. Except
the inconvenient ones
we don't need."

Shall we meet,
someday, our fond
Oppressor, and find
Love, love, only love
and tears, and say
Father (Lord of all
Creation), Savior,

Spirit, Mother,
leaders past and
presented with our
own life (it was
a test, wasn't it—are you
wheat, or tares, are you
willing then,
to follow), and then
Blinded
by the dazzling of
the Love, by the perfect
logic, reason, doctrine,
Truth, finally pure
unadulterated, untranslated
by culture, by prejudice, by
hate upon hate upon—only
love, to feel—
wheat or tares
is a test to see if we will
choose that doctrine first: of love
and love and love and love and love
and see not categories,
races, gender, religion,
classification, ages
culture, finances,
donations, wheat or
tares, but dominion
versus compassion,
and fruits, and how
and whom we choose
to love.

You are lying in bed beside me
Smallest, you are lying in bed beside me
sick fevered after vaccines, at
midnight, and say,"I can still
hear the words Heavenly Father said
in my whole entire mind." I freeze
gently snuggling, casually
ask, "Which words?"
"That we," you say, "were coming
to Earth." We rest for a minute,
nose to nose, until curiosity
gets the better of me. "Were there
other words?" "No,
just that." You yawn, a last memory before
that slender skin between lives, between gateways
of birth, of death, of sleep.
"What does he sound like," I ask,
but you shake your head, scowling
to articulate something you cannot describe
with five year old words, or forty
year ones. "Like an angel
only lower, well
higher and lower. inna middle."
I wonder, my son rarely serious,
rarely still, what other memories you
soon will lose to old age, what
things I don't know of you, be
cause of the clock mortal pushing
us from our soft, nose to nose dusk.

Jargon

Someday, I'm going to want to remember
them in the kitchen talking
about things irl, 360noscope,
Like-Lebron-James.
Sweet Celestia! I know little
what these things mean, but years hence
they will mean today, the
dirty kitchen, walking little feet
and teenage feet,
eating popice and chatting merrily
over whatever game they were so
proud of playing, (was it Minecraft?
Castaways 2?) but have forgotten
years upon years away.
Can I encapsulate
their sweet voices, making
Cheese and egg sandwiches
as mother is too sick
for anything fancy? Listen
they are washing hands
and dishes, talking of weapons,
Being friends, and I,
intrusive,
Loving and loving.

Morning of the last first day

It is a bitter
tangy sweetness to be taking
this last child,
last born, last suckled, last
weaned, last diapered (thank God), last
first words, last first steps, last
first day of kindergarten today dawning . . .
into the car, off to the classroom
hand picked for your struggles
and fallacies, your energetic
lovely, kind teacher, experienced
with small fierce boys
in her thirty years—you will not be her last,
but you are mine, you,
so nervous in changes, timid bravery.
I ask, do you want me
to drop you off or walk you in?
Drop off, you surprise me, I know
where my teacher is.
Maybe sister can walk you in, I
banter, (if not Mama, at least
your first day, not abandoned
to the government, the
system, the next thirteen years
looming like a sunset
like my own personal oceanic view.)
You concede, but no hand holding,
and leave the car having snuggled
her onto the shoulder with your

soft cheek. She reports back—
you faltered once, almost heading
the wrong way, then corrected
steadfast soldier, to march
down the red hallway to that butterfly mobile
which means your door.
You did not stop to hold hands,
but walked ahead, strong,
courageous, not pausing to even
wave goodbye. No tears for you,
my smalllarge
scaredbrave snugglybeastie son

First day, Evening, K5
Your first bus trip, first
full day of school, (well, anywhere)
you arrive home bourn by
the giant belching beast
hurtling itself through the neighborhood
Doors open, you climb out, flushed
from that Augustine pressure cooker.
But as you come across the lawn,
they do not close, but remain
paused, open, waiting.
I think maybe they cannot leave
until you are safely stowed inside—no,
you run in, get water, and we see
they still are paused
on the front lawn, almost,
doors agape.
"Are you ok?" I asked the driver,
who flashes a thumbs up from her phone.
A pause, then answer, "They're stuck,
the doors." "Oh, do you need
WD-40?" Your small self
back strong and straight,
water in hand
marches back towards the bus,
loudly proclaims,
        "I got this."
You stand, and shove
the doors, released,
close majestically before you.

She tests twice, before,
unstuck, she waves and drives
the other children home.
My small Heracles, confident
sits on the step drinking
from your white floral canteen,
wondering why adults make
the simplest things
so difficult.

Lice

There's no shame in it;
some people are just prone
to them, Mama said, after our biweekly
shampoo, rinse, comb, kill cycle
at my aunt's house (double exposure).
The boys had it easy, it was summer
and they practically got shaved.
Mine were worst, scabs where I scratched,
watching movies as my sisters and I
got combed out, each nit caught deftly,
and flick of the comb, twist to inspect, pinch to kill.
flick twist pinch, flick
twist pinch to Mr Wonka, to Juster's animated Which.
I think of this echo
years on, my fear flickering as I drive
(the quick wrenching of my gut, that
heart flicking panic knowing another attack is
coming on). Some people are just
prone to them, my shrink says, as that feeling of
twisting emotions as the anxiety
builds and I
near succumbing to situational stressors.
Of all my sisters
mine are worst, as I successively lose power
to speak to classmates, pizza
delivery guys, neighbors, the phone,
bacterial load increasing
almost to again to scabbing,
I close my eyes, breathe

to release
a technique not effective while driving,
so I quit that, too. These things
just happen, she continues,
we have ways to help you take care
of them; lots of people
have them,
actually, they're just
something people feel
ashamed of, which is silly,
so they don't talk about them. All at once
I am transported to a childhood rinse
in the kitchen sink, a familiar emotional
Pinch.

Persona Non Grata

three years ago, my friend, you
stopped speaking suddenly—
to me, at least—

it happened thus: your son, 12,
teased and taunted at school and
online overseas chat rooms
on his new phone (for which he worked
long hours to afford)
stayed up all night talking
to girlfriends in England,
sleepily bragged
to me.
Hearing alarm bells
I, worried
told you
(shouldn't have,
but did.).
concerned with
newsworthy stories, kidnap,
that unlimited access
to web based super (cult)ure,
might possibly corrupt that
sweetkindsmartyounghardworking
boy, who
to get out of sights, lied
to keep his phone,
more precious than rubies
(shouldn't have
but did.)

You couldn't imagine that I
apparent f(r)iend would stoop
so low. Did you need hate me so
vehemently that no sister/brother
in Christ would accept me, by your word?

and so, now
your boy, forgiving my betrayal
and I (same in return)
counsel on his
pain pornography pot
prescription pain killer,
addictions, fed by those at school
and online. He wishes himself back
before his sports
injuries, his pain managed.
You insist
ibuprofen sufficeth, are confused
by his wild eyes (wouldn't want
him starting any dangerous medicines
long term)—after all, he's
too young to steer
the traps he's foraging to create
for his/your future.
I won't make
that mistake
again,
to let you know
I know
what you may know
part of already.

you're managing
him fine by yourself,
losing him in increments,
lie upon lie
prescription upon precept.

Mare

I finally slept and dreamt
that I was dying, each
mitochondria bursting with
a sound of glass breaking, cell
walls melting (nobody
would believe me). My eyes
black ringed, my limbs, soddenheavy
my mind grossly conflagrated,
and dulled to (with) sleep. To write
became herculean, my body broken
by the heaviness of pens. Each typing
draining life away, the heaviness of holding
remotes, phones, tablets at a
Time, passing, flowing, and I
was old, streaking electric bolts
shooting through my nerves. I woke
and found it true—each surface leveled
collecting dust and books and mold and
patting hands (therethere), it's only
imaginings, you only need a little
nap.

Stand

If you are waiting
to stand
I will stand with you. My space,
my home, I hope,
is made safe for you,
safe for those hidden parts
you didn't think anyone
would desire, safe
for all your lives, your loves, your
sorrows. I try to be safe
daily, walking to and from stores, hooking my ankle
around the strap of my purse under the
table, wishing my daughter
wasn't quite so nice to everyone and
polite as I taught her to be. We need
less sweetness, soft power pedestaled,
more kindness, less bubbling
surface niceties. An increase
in peace, hard fought languishing
over great philosophies of
every gender, slumber parties of thought, learning, ever
learning from voices different than our own.

This
is my vow, America. You want
greatness undefined, but I'm
sitting over here crocheting little
hats to be filled. You want anybody who
speaks their mind—Good. We all
will need a bit more of that
from all sides, less hidden

words sneaking, false interpretation,
in back room discussing, more
transparency in truth
and lies. When someone tells you who they are,
believe them.
When we stand, maybe with a cane, maybe in our chairs,
if you want
to stand with me, my arm
will be around you,
Not shoving you away
Not pushing you down
Not pushing my hands against ears and saying
your words do not count because
We all count. Not our votes, maybe,
but our voices, our words,
our loud typing. Truth unpresidented,
unprecedented, unpredictable, impressively uncovered
and held
to light, torch passage—
an interesting studied specimen.
We will not turn our eyes
from that horrorugliness
as triage is needful, and medics
want often to flee from horror, but
refuse.

I refuse.

We'll face together, seeing that
face of sunset, knowing
rose sun rises after absence, and I
have got all night
to work.

Hard

I get it, now.
I hear you, and I'm so
very sorry.
It must be
so frustrating to wake
and see your friends (you thought
them friends) blaming you for this
mess. Just because you fit
some after-poll demographic that
might have caused some maybe
indiscreet actions. Your
vote was different. I know you. It must
be hard to be blamed
for the actions of a few
neo-nazis empowered, just because
of the color of your own skin. You'd never
spray paint swastikas or threaten
disabledminoritieswomenreligions.
I get it, now. You'd never write
that note calling someone a
fag, or scream "n*****" at a
child online or on the street. It's not
who you are. That would be
mean, and you,
I *know* you, and you are
not mean. And it's totally
completely wrong
for someone to blame you for
the downfall of Western Society, just

because your own peaceful religion has
some freaky fundamentalist outliers who
think their own extreme
ly rigid interpretation of
scripture is the one true
way. That is
Not who you are.
I get it. It must
be hard, and America, I'm
so very, very sorry.

Love is
love is
love. We humans have
'most every culture distinct
trouble defining this
small thing, and yet say,
defensive, which cannot
qualify in present
colonial society (whichever
that may be in this
century and hemisphere)—I'm no
different: I see false
love, feigned love, all around me. All of these
toxic, poisoned well, controlling
coercive loves, holding
tight, manipulation continual of
words, of thought, denial
of feelings, denial of experience, denial
of psychology, denial of truth. This not
being specific to gender, to
sexuality, this dangerous
masked robber of love,
Hiding in three little words, hiding
unspecified to agereligion, racenationality,
incomesexuality, in
decrepitude creeping, grinding dreams,
Milling souls like flour,
olives in a press.
There cannot anything compare with these: false
love, faked love, feigned
Love, currency devalued. If paper

bills, counterfeit, are discovered, we burn
efficiently, brand those
creators criminal. But real
love, is lovely, not alone
there for prosperity, posterity, nor any
one outside to conjure or comprehend
without that love. I myself might find
the very concept of the loving
(kissingintimate)
between my friend and her
husband, my friend and her
wife, disgusting, and neither is that counterfeit
branding of love, but mine
in judgement for them, not finding
their faces, their bodies
attractive to my own preference?
Nor family pretended, whether biologically
babies come gifted from within, or gifted
from without their bodies, (or not at all),
IVF, test tube, or otherwise
surrogated, or none, by choice or
biology. Love is love,
Is love, rejecting
all conceptual counterfeit, rejoicing
in lives, in kindness,
mercy, compassion—that atoning
love cannot possibly be counter
to the understanding of God's universe,
regardless of those liveloving, if indeed
violence spiritual, financial, emotional
is not. (But it is.)

J.

I'm not sure,
did he ever even
Love me, ever?
I pause at her tear
torn face and think
there might be no
comfort left to go with the
no more love, the lack, utterly
devoid of empathy.
He is gathering
legions of flying monkies
testifying of her
laziness, her inability to
nurture as he would have her
nurture, teach as he would choose
her to teach.
I'm beginning, she continues
to question everything. Everything!
a pause.
Except for Christ's love? Is it real? Am I (whispered)
losing my faith?

I think suddenly of my own,
skim skipping across
sparklingcrisp lake waters high
in the Rockies, skidding
Tossed—gravity conquered—
falling, falling, fallen
darker darkened current tossed, flowing ever
flowing toward the sea.

Smoothed, smothered,
nibbled upon by fish and ducks,
resting nightward wishing
for merry skimming, until,
awaking to depths, sea
creatures, monsters I was
taught to fear—and they
are creatures just like those that threw
me long ago: the depths have peace,
and time to see both starfish and
the stars.

Moldy
Remember when we used
to find comfort in the mold,
the talk of happy
families, happy children, happy
homes if only you
will follow just this little
checklist? And we posted
it next to our lives, and checked
it often, and did
Everything upon it. And
we should have been
everything promised—
Simple math! If/Then
theorem. If this,
then this. Remember
when we realized we
did not fit the checklist and
scrabbled trying to
editrevisedouble
check, as surely
there was something
we had missed or surely
it would be Better. When
the babies grew a little, when
the children are older, when the
car is fixed, when your job is
closer and has less
hours, when we are paid
more, when I hurt less,

And here I am
with the sudden recognition
it is never going to get better
with that checklist on the wall.

Intent to File
The spider picks
apart her home,
web dismantling
broken strands, wadding
ripped bits, devouring,
web devouring, delicate,
strong. She will form anew
in her filled abdomen
the ropes she must climb
attach climb, inventing
new connections, creating
acrobatic formations,
birthing homes, jobs, lively
hoods, while I sit
unraveling.

Acknowledgements

I would like to thank Segullah for over a decade ago reading one of my poems and thinking, "Huh. we could print this," instead of "Good grief, what drivel." I would like to thank all of my early readers, especially my friends from the FMH boards, all of whom I'm reticent to name because I'll miss someone. Several of you have poems here brought to being from your thoughts or works, and I'm continually grateful for your thinking and sparking new ideas in my sluggish mind. Your work inspires my work. Kristen Shill has blessed me both with her unflagging friendship, and with numerous writing prompts. Without her continual sharing of poetry back and forth this book would not have been possible. I'm terribly grateful for my sisters, Cara, Mary, and Naomi, without whom Harrishood would be bland and dismal, and who always lift me towards my goals, especially when I am set about by millstones and albatrosses. I'd like to thank anyone who suffered through my poetry in middle school, with horrifyingly overwrought metaphors. Hopefully I've improved. No promises, though.

You are all my treasures, and I love all of you. Really.

HEATHER HARRIS BERGEVIN is a Southern author who also happens to be LDS. Her parents named her Heather because it's a weed that grows in difficult places, but manages to bloom anyway, which is generally her goal. In her free time, she . . . nope, she has no free time, because she's a mom, a student, and chronically ill. Most of her education was at BYU, but she's finishing at the University of South Carolina, which actually is a pretty good metaphor for her life. Heather is in love with learning art, music, science, history, and with life, all of which love has been hard fought. She loves her three brilliant children more than all of these other things combined. Heather fidgets by writing poems and drawing zentangles, and is surprisedly delighted when people like either or both. She loves it when people laugh at, or indeed even get, her snarky little jokes.

Made in the USA
San Bernardino, CA
26 April 2019